Sustainability in Germany

Contents

Sustainability in Germany

Anurag Anurag

1

Pioneering Waste Management and Recycling

Germany is widely regarded as a global leader in waste management and recycling, setting high standards through its innovative and efficient systems. The country's approach to waste management is characterized by a comprehensive framework that emphasizes reduction, reuse, and recycling, aiming to minimize environmental impact and promote sustainability.

At the core of Germany's waste management strategy is the principle of waste hierarchy, which prioritizes waste prevention and resource efficiency. This hierarchy is reflected in various legislative measures and initiatives that encourage businesses and consumers to adopt more sustainable practices. One of the key components of this strategy is the Circular Economy Act, which aims to create a closed-loop system where products and materials are continually reused and recycled, reducing the need for new raw materials.

Germany's success in waste management can be attributed to its robust infrastructure and advanced technologies. The country boasts an extensive network of recycling facilities, waste-to-energy plants, and composting sites, all of which play a crucial role in processing different types of waste. These facilities are equipped with state-of-the-art technologies that ensure efficient sorting, treatment, and recovery of valuable materials. For instance, automated sorting systems use advanced sensors and robotics to separate recyclable materials with high precision, maximizing recovery rates and minimizing contamination.

One of the most notable aspects of Germany's waste management system is its high recycling rates. The country has achieved impressive recycling rates through a combination of mandatory recycling laws, effective public awareness campaigns, and convenient recycling infrastructure. The dual system, introduced in the 1990s, requires manufacturers and retailers to take responsibility for the packaging waste they produce. This system is managed by dual system operators who ensure that packaging waste is collected, sorted, and recycled, significantly reducing the volume of waste sent to landfills.

In addition to packaging waste, Germany has implemented successful recycling programs for other types of waste, such as electronic waste (e-waste), organic waste, and construction and demolition waste. E-waste recycling, for example, is facilitated through designated collection points where consumers can dispose of their old electronics. These items are then transported to specialized facilities where valuable metals and components are extracted and reused. Similarly, organic waste is collected separately and processed in composting facilities or anaerobic digestion plants to produce biogas and nutrient-rich compost, which can be used in agriculture.

Public participation and awareness are critical to the effectiveness of Germany's waste management and recycling systems. The government, along with non-governmental organizations, conducts extensive educational campaigns to inform citizens about the importance of waste separation and recycling. Schools and community groups are actively involved in promoting recycling practices, fostering a culture of environmental responsibility from an early age. Additionally, the availability of well-designed recycling bins and clear labeling makes it easy for residents to sort their waste correctly.

Germany's waste management and recycling efforts also extend to the industrial sector. The country has implemented stringent regulations that require industries to adopt sustainable waste management practices. Companies are encouraged to minimize waste generation through process optimization, material substitution, and efficient resource use. Industrial symbiosis, where waste from one industry serves as a raw material for another, is also promoted, further enhancing resource efficiency and reducing waste.

Looking ahead, Germany continues to innovate and improve its waste management and recycling systems. Research and development efforts focus on finding new ways to recover and recycle materials, improve waste treatment technologies, and develop sustainable packaging solutions. The country's commitment to a circular economy is evident in its ongoing efforts to create a more sustainable and resilient waste management system that can adapt to changing environmental and economic conditions.

In conclusion, Germany's pioneering approach to waste management and recycling demonstrates how comprehensive policies, advanced technologies, and active public participation can effectively address the challenges of waste and resource management. By continually striving for innovation and efficiency, Germany sets an exemplary model for other nations aiming to achieve high recycling rates and sustainable waste management practices.

2

Sustainable Transportation - Green Mobility Shift

Germany is at the forefront of sustainable transportation, leading a green mobility shift aimed at reducing emissions, improving air quality, and fostering innovation in the transportation sector. This chapter examines Germany's comprehensive efforts to promote electric vehicles, enhance public transportation systems, and encourage low-emission travel.

Germany's commitment to electric vehicles (EVs) is a central pillar of its sustainable transportation strategy. The government has implemented various incentives to accelerate the adoption of EVs, including purchase subsidies, tax benefits, and investment in charging infrastructure. These measures have significantly increased the number of EVs on German roads, positioning the country as a leader in the electric mobility revolution.

To support the widespread use of EVs, Germany is rapidly expanding its network of charging stations. This includes high-speed chargers along highways and more accessible charging points in urban areas and residential neighborhoods. Public and private sector partnerships have been crucial in developing this infrastructure, ensuring that EV owners have convenient and reliable access to charging facilities.

In addition to promoting electric vehicles, Germany is committed to strengthening its public transportation system as a sustainable and efficient alternative to private car use. Investments in public transport aim to make it more accessible, reliable, and attractive to commuters. The expansion and modernization of rail networks, buses, and trams are central to this effort. High-speed trains, such as the ICE (InterCity Express), connect major cities, reducing travel times and providing a viable alternative to domestic air travel.

Germany's cities are also implementing innovative solutions to enhance urban mobility. Many cities are expanding their cycling infrastructure, including dedicated bike lanes, bike-sharing programs, and secure parking facilities. These initiatives not only promote healthier lifestyles but also reduce congestion and emissions in urban areas. Berlin, for example, has implemented an extensive bike-sharing system that integrates seamlessly with its public transportation network, encouraging residents and tourists to choose sustainable modes of travel.

Low-emission zones (LEZs) are another key component of Germany's strategy to reduce urban air pollution. These zones restrict access to vehicles that do not meet specific emission standards, effectively reducing the number of high-polluting cars in city centers. LEZs have been implemented in several major cities, including Berlin, Hamburg, and Munich, contributing to significant improvements in air quality and public health.

Germany's automotive industry, renowned for its innovation and engineering excellence, is also playing a crucial role in the green mobility shift. Leading manufacturers, such as Volkswagen, BMW, and Daimler, are investing heavily in the development of electric and hybrid vehicles. These companies are also exploring new technologies, such as hydrogen fuel cells and autonomous driving, to further advance sustainable transportation.

The integration of digital technologies is transforming the transportation landscape in Germany. Smart mobility solutions, such as real-time traffic management systems, ride-sharing platforms, and mobility-as-a-service (MaaS) applications, are making transportation more efficient and user-friendly. These technologies enable better coordination between different modes of transport, optimize routes, and provide users with seamless, door-to-door travel experiences.

Public engagement and education are essential to the success of Germany's sustainable transportation initiatives. The government and non-governmental organizations conduct campaigns to raise awareness about the benefits of sustainable travel and encourage behavioral changes. Programs in schools and communities teach the importance of reducing one's carbon footprint and provide practical tips for incorporating sustainable practices into daily life.

Germany's efforts to promote sustainable transportation are also supported by robust policy frameworks and international collaborations. The National Platform for Electric Mobility (NPE), for example, brings together stakeholders from industry, government, and academia to coordinate and advance the country's electric mobility agenda. Germany also participates in European Union initiatives and global partnerships to share best practices and drive collective action on sustainable transportation.

Looking to the future, Germany's green mobility shift continues to evolve, with ongoing research and development aimed at further reducing emissions and enhancing transportation efficiency. Innovations in battery technology, renewable energy integration, and intelligent transportation systems will play a vital role in shaping the future of sustainable mobility.

In conclusion, Germany's comprehensive approach to sustainable transportation reflects a deep commitment to reducing emissions, improving public health, and fostering innovation. Through the promotion of electric vehicles, the enhancement of public transportation, and the encouragement of low-emission travel, Germany is setting a high standard for sustainable mobility and paving the way for a greener, more sustainable future.

3

Green Architecture and Urban Planning

Germany stands at the forefront of sustainable construction and urban planning, setting global standards through innovative practices and energy-efficient designs. This chapter explores the principles, methodologies, and implementations that make Germany a leader in green architecture and urban planning, highlighting the country's commitment to creating sustainable, livable, and resilient urban environments.

At the heart of Germany's approach to sustainable construction is the concept of energy efficiency. German architects and builders prioritize designs that minimize energy consumption while maximizing the use of renewable energy sources. This focus is evident in the widespread adoption of Passivhaus (Passive House) standards, which set rigorous criteria for energy efficiency, comfort, and affordability. Passivhaus buildings use superinsulation, advanced window technologies, and airtight construction to drastically reduce heating and cooling energy needs, often achieving energy savings of up to 90% compared to conventional buildings.

Innovative building materials and construction techniques play a crucial role in Germany's green architecture. The use of sustainable, locally sourced materials, such as timber, recycled steel, and natural insulation, reduces the environmental impact of construction. Green roofs and facades, which are increasingly common in German cities, provide insulation, reduce urban heat island effects, and promote biodiversity. These living structures not only enhance the aesthetic appeal of buildings but also contribute to improved air quality and stormwater management.

Germany's urban planning strategies emphasize the integration of green spaces and sustainable infrastructure. Cities like Freiburg and Hamburg are renowned for their comprehensive urban development plans that prioritize walkability, public transportation, and mixed-use development. These cities incorporate extensive networks of parks, green corridors, and urban forests, creating healthier and more resilient urban environments. By integrating nature into the urban fabric, these planning efforts enhance the quality of life for residents and promote environmental sustainability.

Public transportation and cycling infrastructure are key components of Germany's sustainable urban planning. Efficient and accessible public transport systems reduce reliance on private vehicles, decreasing traffic congestion and emissions. Cities invest in extensive tram, bus, and train networks that connect neighborhoods and promote sustainable mobility. Cycling is also heavily promoted, with dedicated bike lanes, bike-sharing programs, and secure parking facilities making it a convenient and popular mode of transport.

Energy-efficient buildings are central to Germany's sustainability goals. The Energy Saving Ordinance (EnEV) and the Renewable Energy Heat Act (EEWärmeG) set stringent standards for new constructions and renovations, ensuring that buildings contribute to national energy and climate targets. High-performance building envelopes, efficient heating and cooling systems, and the integration of renewable energy sources, such as solar panels and geothermal heat pumps, are standard features of modern German buildings.

The implementation of smart technologies further enhances the efficiency and sustainability of Germany's built environment. Smart grids, energy management systems, and intelligent building controls optimize energy use and enhance the resilience of energy systems. Buildings equipped with sensors and automation can adapt to changing conditions, improving comfort and reducing energy consumption. These technologies enable more efficient use of resources and support the transition to a low-carbon economy.

Germany's commitment to sustainable construction and urban planning extends beyond technical solutions to include social and economic considerations. Community engagement and participatory planning processes ensure that development projects meet the needs and preferences of local residents. Affordable housing initiatives and mixed-income developments promote social equity and inclusivity, ensuring that sustainable urban environments are accessible to all.

Education and research are vital to advancing Germany's leadership in green architecture and urban planning. Universities and research institutions collaborate with industry and government to develop new technologies, materials, and design strategies. Training programs for architects, engineers, and planners emphasize sustainability principles and foster a culture of innovation and excellence in the construction sector.

In conclusion, Germany's approach to green architecture and urban planning demonstrates how sustainable construction practices and energy-efficient buildings can create vibrant, resilient, and livable urban environments. By prioritizing energy efficiency, innovative materials, green spaces, and smart technologies, Germany sets a global benchmark for sustainable development. These efforts not only contribute to environmental protection but also enhance the quality of life for residents, ensuring a sustainable future for generations to come.

4

Leadership in Climate Policy

Germany has established itself as a global leader in climate policy, actively shaping international climate agreements and implementing comprehensive domestic climate action plans. This chapter examines Germany's influential role in global climate policy and the various measures it has adopted to mitigate climate change and transition to a low-carbon economy.

Germany's commitment to addressing climate change is deeply embedded in its policy framework and international diplomacy. As a member of the European Union and various international organizations, Germany has been instrumental in driving ambitious climate targets and fostering collaborative efforts to combat global warming. One of the key platforms for Germany's climate leadership is the United Nations Framework Convention on Climate Change (UNFCCC), where Germany has consistently advocated for strong, binding commitments to reduce greenhouse gas emissions.

The Paris Agreement, adopted in 2015, marks a significant milestone in global climate policy, with Germany playing a pivotal role in its negotiation and subsequent implementation. The agreement sets out a global framework to limit global warming to well below 2 degrees Celsius, with efforts to limit the temperature increase to 1.5 degrees Celsius. Germany's leadership was crucial in shaping the agreement's ambitious targets and in mobilizing financial and technical support for developing countries to achieve their climate goals.

Domestically, Germany's climate policy is guided by the Climate Action Plan 2050, which outlines the country's long-term strategy to achieve greenhouse gas neutrality by mid-century. The plan sets interim targets for 2030, including a 55% reduction in greenhouse gas emissions compared to 1990 levels. It encompasses various sectors such as energy, industry, transportation, buildings, and agriculture, each with specific measures and milestones to ensure progress towards decarbonization.

In the energy sector, Germany's Energiewende, or energy transition, is a cornerstone of its climate policy. This ambitious initiative aims to shift the energy system from fossil fuels to renewable energy sources, significantly reducing emissions and enhancing energy security. The Renewable Energy Sources Act (EEG) has been instrumental in promoting wind, solar, and biomass energy, making Germany a global leader in renewable energy capacity. The phase-out of nuclear power, coupled with the gradual reduction of coal-fired power plants, underscores Germany's commitment to a sustainable energy future.

The transportation sector, a major source of greenhouse gas emissions, is also a focal point of Germany's climate action. The government promotes the adoption of electric vehicles (EVs) through subsidies, tax incentives, and investment in charging infrastructure. Public transportation systems are being expanded and modernized, with a focus on low-emission and zero-emission technologies. Additionally, policies to enhance cycling infrastructure and promote sustainable urban mobility are integral to reducing transportation-related emissions.

Germany's building sector is another critical area for climate mitigation. The Energy Saving Ordinance (EnEV) and the Renewable Energy Heat Act (EEWärmeG) set stringent standards for new buildings and renovations to improve energy efficiency and increase the use of renewable energy. Programs like the Energy Efficiency Incentive Program (APEE) provide financial support for energy-saving measures in residential and commercial buildings, contributing to significant reductions in energy consumption and emissions.

In the industrial sector, Germany emphasizes the importance of innovation and technology to achieve climate goals. The government supports research and development in clean technologies, energy-efficient processes, and sustainable materials. Initiatives like the Hydrogen Strategy aim to develop a robust hydrogen economy, leveraging green hydrogen as a key component of the energy transition and industrial decarbonization.

Germany's climate policy also encompasses measures to enhance climate resilience and adaptation. Recognizing the impacts of climate change on ecosystems, infrastructure, and communities, the German Adaptation Strategy (DAS) outlines actions to reduce vulnerability and increase resilience to climate-related risks. This includes investments in flood protection, sustainable agriculture practices, and the conservation of biodiversity and natural habitats.

Internationally, Germany continues to lead by example and support global climate action. Through the International Climate Initiative (IKI), Germany funds projects in developing and emerging countries to promote sustainable development, reduce emissions, and enhance climate resilience. Germany's contributions to the Green Climate Fund and other multilateral climate finance mechanisms demonstrate its commitment to helping vulnerable nations cope with the impacts of climate change and transition to low-carbon economies.

Public engagement and participation are essential components of Germany's climate policy. The government collaborates with non-governmental organizations, businesses, and citizens to raise awareness and foster a culture of sustainability. Educational programs, public campaigns, and stakeholder dialogues ensure that climate action is a shared responsibility, with broad support across society.

In conclusion, Germany's leadership in climate policy is characterized by its proactive role in shaping international agreements, implementing comprehensive domestic measures, and fostering global cooperation. By setting ambitious targets, investing in renewable energy and sustainable technologies, and supporting vulnerable countries, Germany exemplifies the commitment and innovation needed to address the global climate crisis. These efforts not only contribute to mitigating climate change but also pave the way for a sustainable and resilient future for all.

5

Towards a Circular Economy

G ermany has been a pioneer in the development and implementation of circular economy principles, emphasizing the reduction of
waste, and the promotion of the reuse and recycling of materials. This

chapter delves into the various initiatives, policies, and practices that underscore Germany's commitment to creating a sustainable and efficient circular economy. A circular economy aims to keep resources in use for as long as possible, extracting maximum value from them before recovering and regenerating materials at the end of their service life. Germany's approach to achieving this involves a multifaceted strategy that includes legislative measures, innovative technologies, public engagement, and international collaboration.

Central to Germany's circular economy is a robust legislative framework that supports sustainable waste management and resource efficiency. The Circular Economy Act (Kreislaufwirtschaftsgesetz), first introduced in 1996 and subsequently updated, serves as the cornerstone of these efforts. This legislation sets the hierarchy for waste management: prevention, reuse, recycling, and disposal. It mandates that waste should be managed in a way that conserves resources and protects human health and the environment. The Packaging Act (Verpackungsgesetz), effective from 2019, builds on this framework by introducing stricter recycling quotas for packaging materials and requiring producers to register with a central authority. The act aims to reduce packaging waste and ensure that packaging materials are designed for recyclability.

Germany's waste prevention strategies focus on reducing the generation of waste at its source. The government promotes eco-design principles, encouraging manufacturers to create products that are durable, repairable, and recyclable. Extended producer responsibility (EPR) schemes require producers to take back their products at the end of their life cycle, ensuring proper disposal and recycling. Resource efficiency is another key aspect of Germany's circular economy initiatives. The National Programme for Sustainable Consumption encourages consumers to make environmentally friendly choices, while the Resource Efficiency Programme (ProgRess) aims to decouple economic growth from resource use. ProgRess focuses on improving resource efficiency across all sectors of the economy, promoting innovations in product design, manufacturing processes, and recycling technologies.

Germany boasts one of the highest recycling rates in the world, thanks to its comprehensive recycling infrastructure and public participation. The dual system, established in the early 1990s, separates packaging waste from other types of waste, ensuring efficient sorting and recycling. This system is managed by dual system operators who coordinate the collection, sorting, and recycling of packaging waste. Municipal waste management systems are equally robust, with local authorities providing separate bins for paper, glass, plastic, and organic waste. Advanced sorting facilities use cutting-edge technologies, such as optical sensors and automated sorting machines, to separate recyclable materials with high precision. These efforts have significantly reduced the volume of waste sent to landfills and increased the recovery of valuable materials.

Electronic waste (e-waste) recycling is another area where Germany excels. Designated collection points and take-back schemes for e-waste ensure that discarded electronics are properly recycled. Specialized recycling facilities dismantle and process e-waste to recover precious metals, plastics, and other materials, reducing the need for virgin resources. Industrial symbiosis, where waste or by-products from one industry serve as raw materials for another, is a key component of Germany's circular economy. This approach promotes the efficient use of resources and reduces waste by creating a network of interconnected industries that benefit from each other's waste streams.

Public engagement and education are crucial to the success of Germany's circular economy. The government, along with non-governmental organizations, conducts extensive campaigns to raise awareness about waste reduction, recycling, and sustainable consumption. Schools and universities integrate circular economy principles into their curricula, fostering a culture of sustainability from an early age. Additionally, community programs and local initiatives encourage citizens to participate actively in recycling and waste management efforts.

Germany's commitment to a circular economy is also evident in its research and innovation efforts. Universities, research institutions, and private companies collaborate on projects aimed at developing new materials, recycling technologies, and sustainable product designs. Government funding supports these initiatives, ensuring that Germany remains at the forefront of circular economy innovations. The country's leadership in this field extends to the international arena, where Germany shares its expertise and collaborates with other nations to promote global sustainability.

In conclusion, Germany's approach to a circular economy demonstrates how comprehensive policies, innovative technologies, and active public engagement can create a sustainable and efficient system of resource use. By prioritizing waste prevention, promoting recycling, and encouraging the reuse of materials, Germany sets an exemplary model for other countries to follow. These efforts not only protect the environment but also drive economic growth and innovation, ensuring a sustainable future for generations to come.

6

Biodiversity and Conservation

Germany has long been a leader in environmental protection, particularly in the areas of biodiversity conservation and the preservation of natural landscapes. This chapter provides a detailed examination of Germany's comprehensive conservation programs and the multifaceted approaches it employs to protect its rich natural heritage.

Germany's commitment to biodiversity is rooted in a robust legal framework that includes national, regional, and international regulations. At the national level, the Federal Nature Conservation Act (Bundesnaturschutzgesetz) serves as the cornerstone of conservation policy. This act sets the principles for the protection, maintenance, and development of nature and landscapes, emphasizing the importance of biodiversity for ecosystem health and human well-being.

Germany is home to a diverse array of ecosystems, including forests, wetlands, grasslands, and coastal areas, each supporting a wide range of species. The country's conservation efforts are aimed at preserving these habitats through a network of protected areas. These include 16 national parks, 105 nature parks, and numerous biosphere reserves and nature reserves. These protected areas cover approximately 15% of the country's land area, providing safe havens for many species and maintaining ecological processes.

One of Germany's flagship conservation programs is the Natura 2000 network, which is part of the European Union's strategy to protect Europe's most valuable and threatened species and habitats. Germany has designated over 5,000 Natura 2000 sites, encompassing a variety of habitats such as forests, heathlands, rivers, and coastal areas. These sites are managed to ensure the long-term survival of Europe's most precious biodiversity, balancing conservation with human activities.

Forest conservation is a significant focus of Germany's biodiversity efforts. Forests cover about one-third of the country's land area, providing critical habitat for wildlife, regulating the climate, and offering recreational opportunities. Sustainable forest management practices are implemented to maintain the ecological integrity of these forests. This includes selective logging, reforestation, and the protection of old-growth forests. Germany's Forest Strategy 2020 aims to enhance the resilience of forests to climate change, promote biodiversity, and ensure sustainable use of forest resources.

Wetland and water body conservation is another priority. Wetlands play a crucial role in water purification, flood regulation, and providing habitat for many species. Germany has several Ramsar sites, wetlands of international importance, designated under the Ramsar Convention. Efforts to restore and protect wetlands include re-wetting drained peatlands, rehabilitating river floodplains, and managing water levels to mimic natural hydrological cycles. These actions help to preserve wetland biodiversity and enhance ecosystem services.

Grasslands and agricultural landscapes are also key areas for conservation. Traditional agricultural practices, such as extensive grazing and mowing, have created species-rich meadows and pastures. Germany supports agri-environmental schemes that incentivize farmers to maintain these practices, promoting biodiversity while ensuring agricultural productivity. These schemes include financial support for organic farming, the creation of flower strips, and the maintenance of hedgerows and other landscape features that provide habitat for wildlife.

Germany's conservation efforts are not limited to terrestrial ecosystems. The country also works to protect marine biodiversity in the North Sea and Baltic Sea. Marine protected areas have been established to safeguard important habitats such as reefs, sandbanks, and sea grass beds. Measures to reduce overfishing, limit bycatch, and prevent marine pollution are implemented to ensure the health of marine ecosystems and the species they support.

Public engagement and education are integral to Germany's biodiversity conservation strategy. Conservation organizations, such as the German Nature Conservation Union (NABU) and the World Wide Fund for Nature (WWF) Germany, play a vital role in raising awareness and involving citizens in conservation activities. Programs and campaigns promote the importance of biodiversity and encourage actions such as citizen science projects, habitat restoration, and sustainable consumption.

Research and monitoring are essential components of Germany's conservation efforts. Universities, research institutions, and government agencies conduct studies on species and habitats, assess the effectiveness of conservation measures, and develop new approaches to biodiversity protection. Monitoring programs track the status of species and ecosystems, providing data that inform conservation planning and policy decisions.

Germany also plays a significant role in international biodiversity conservation. The country is a party to numerous international agreements, such as the Convention on Biological Diversity (CBD) and the Convention on Migratory Species (CMS). Through these agreements, Germany collaborates with other nations to address global biodiversity challenges, share knowledge and best practices, and support conservation projects worldwide.

In conclusion, Germany's approach to biodiversity and conservation is comprehensive and multifaceted, involving legal frameworks, protected areas, sustainable management practices, public engagement, research, and international cooperation. These efforts reflect a deep commitment to preserving the natural world for future generations, ensuring that Germany's rich biodiversity and natural landscapes continue to thrive.

7

Community Engagement and Grassroots Movements

Germany's commitment to sustainability extends beyond government policies and corporate initiatives, encompassing a vibrant landscape of community engagement and grassroots movements. These local efforts play a crucial role in driving environmental awareness and action, fostering a culture of sustainability from the ground up. This chapter explores various community initiatives and grassroots movements that are making significant contributions to sustainability in Germany.

Local community initiatives in Germany are diverse and widespread, addressing a range of environmental issues from energy conservation and waste reduction to biodiversity preservation and climate action. These initiatives often arise from a shared recognition of the importance of protecting the environment and improving quality of life at the local level. Community gardens, energy cooperatives, and zero-waste projects are just a few examples of how local groups are making a difference.

One notable example of community engagement is the widespread network of community gardens (Gemeinschaftsgärten) across Germany. These gardens provide urban residents with the opportunity to grow their own food, learn about sustainable agriculture, and foster social connections. Community gardens not only contribute to local food security but also enhance urban biodiversity and create green spaces that improve air quality and reduce urban heat islands. They serve as educational hubs where residents can learn about composting, permaculture, and other sustainable practices.

Energy cooperatives (Energiegenossenschaften) are another powerful example of grassroots movements driving sustainability in Germany. These cooperatives are formed by local residents who collectively invest in renewable energy projects, such as wind turbines and solar panels. By pooling resources, members of energy cooperatives can generate and use clean energy, reducing their reliance on fossil fuels and contributing to the local economy. Energy cooperatives empower communities to take control of their energy supply, promote energy democracy, and foster a sense of ownership and responsibility for local energy production.

Zero-waste initiatives are gaining momentum in Germany, driven by community groups dedicated to reducing waste and promoting circular economy principles. These initiatives include zero-waste stores, repair cafes, and clothing swaps, which encourage the reuse and recycling of materials and products. Zero-waste stores offer package-free shopping options, allowing customers to bring their own containers and reduce single-use packaging. Repair cafes provide a space for community members to bring broken items and learn how to fix them, extending the lifespan of products and reducing waste. Clothing swaps promote the reuse of garments, reducing the environmental impact of fast fashion.

Grassroots movements in Germany are also at the forefront of climate action, advocating for policies and practices that mitigate climate change and protect the environment. Fridays for Future, a youth-led movement inspired by climate activist Greta Thunberg, has mobilized thousands of young people across Germany to demand stronger climate policies and actions. Through regular climate strikes and demonstrations, Fridays for Future has raised public awareness about the urgency of addressing climate change and influenced political discourse on environmental issues.

Extinction Rebellion, another grassroots movement, employs non-violent civil disobedience to draw attention to the climate and ecological crises. By organizing protests, blockades, and public art installations, Extinction Rebellion aims to pressure governments and institutions to take immediate and decisive action to address environmental degradation and prevent biodiversity loss. Their efforts have sparked widespread discussions about the need for systemic change and the role of civil society in driving environmental action.

Local initiatives and grassroots movements often collaborate with municipal governments, businesses, and non-governmental organizations to amplify their impact. These partnerships enable the sharing of resources, knowledge, and expertise, creating synergies that enhance the effectiveness of sustainability efforts. Municipal governments, for example, may support community projects through funding, infrastructure, or policy changes that facilitate sustainable practices.

Education and awareness-raising are central to the success of community engagement and grassroots movements. Environmental education programs, workshops, and public campaigns help to inform and inspire citizens to adopt sustainable behaviors and participate in local initiatives. Schools, universities, and community centers play a crucial role in delivering these educational efforts, fostering a culture of sustainability among people of all ages.

In conclusion, community engagement and grassroots movements are vital components of Germany's sustainability landscape. Through local initiatives, energy cooperatives, zero-waste projects, and climate activism, these efforts empower individuals and communities to take meaningful action towards environmental protection and sustainability. By fostering collaboration, education, and a shared sense of responsibility, community engagement and grassroots movements contribute significantly to Germany's overall environmental goals, demonstrating the power of collective action in driving positive change.

8

Challenges and Innovations

Germany's commitment to sustainability is robust, yet the journey towards a fully sustainable future is fraught with significant challenges.

Addressing these challenges requires continuous innovation and adaptation. This chapter explores the key obstacles Germany faces in its sustainability efforts and highlights the innovative solutions being developed to overcome them.

One of the primary challenges in Germany's sustainability journey is the transition from fossil fuels to renewable energy sources. While the Energiewende (energy transition) has made significant strides, integrating a high share of renewable energy into the power grid poses technical and logistical difficulties. Renewable energy sources like wind and solar are intermittent, requiring advancements in energy storage and grid management to ensure a reliable and stable energy supply. Germany is investing heavily in battery storage technologies and smart grid solutions to address these issues. Innovations such as large-scale battery farms, pumped hydro storage, and vehicle-to-grid systems are being explored to store excess energy generated during peak production times and release it during periods of high demand.

Another challenge is the decarbonization of the industrial sector, which is a significant contributor to Germany's greenhouse gas emissions. Industries such as steel, cement, and chemicals are energy-intensive and rely heavily on fossil fuels. To mitigate emissions, Germany is investing in green hydrogen technology. Green hydrogen, produced using renewable energy, offers a promising solution for decarbonizing industrial processes. Pilot projects and research initiatives are underway to develop cost-effective methods for producing, storing, and transporting green hydrogen, aiming to replace fossil fuels in industrial applications.

The transportation sector also presents substantial challenges. Despite progress in promoting electric vehicles (EVs), transitioning the entire transportation system to sustainable modes of travel is complex. Germany faces hurdles in expanding EV infrastructure, including the availability of charging stations and the development of fast-charging technology. To address this, the government is supporting the installation of a comprehensive network of public and private charging stations, particularly in urban areas and along highways. Furthermore, advancements in battery technology, such as solid-state batteries, are being pursued to increase the range and reduce the charging time of EVs.

In urban areas, balancing sustainable development with the needs of growing populations poses significant challenges. Cities must manage issues related to air quality, traffic congestion, and housing shortages while promoting sustainable urban planning. Germany is implementing smart city initiatives that leverage digital technologies to enhance urban living. These initiatives include intelligent traffic management systems, energy-efficient buildings with integrated renewable energy sources, and urban mobility solutions like bike-sharing programs and electric public transport. By creating more sustainable and livable urban environments, these innovations aim to address the complex demands of urbanization.

Waste management and recycling remain critical areas where Germany continues to innovate. Despite high recycling rates, challenges such as plastic pollution and the need for a circular economy persist. Germany is pioneering advanced recycling technologies, including chemical recycling, which can process mixed and contaminated plastics that are difficult to recycle mechanically. These technologies break down plastics into their chemical components, allowing them to be reused in the production of new materials. Additionally, initiatives to promote a circular economy, such as extended producer responsibility (EPR) schemes and eco-design standards, encourage manufacturers to design products that are easier to recycle and have a longer lifespan.

Climate change adaptation is another significant challenge, requiring innovative approaches to enhance resilience. Germany is experiencing increased frequency and intensity of extreme weather events, such as floods and heatwaves. To mitigate these impacts, Germany is investing in nature-based solutions and green infrastructure. Projects include the restoration of wetlands and floodplains to enhance natural water retention, the creation of green roofs and walls to reduce urban heat, and the development of resilient agricultural practices. These measures not only protect communities but also promote biodiversity and ecosystem services.

Public engagement and education are essential to the success of Germany's sustainability initiatives. However, fostering widespread behavioral change and public participation remains challenging. Innovative approaches to environmental education and awareness campaigns are being implemented to address this. Interactive platforms, social media, and community-based projects are used to engage citizens and promote sustainable lifestyles. Schools and universities are integrating sustainability into their curricula, encouraging the next generation to prioritize environmental stewardship.

International collaboration is crucial for addressing global sustainability challenges. Germany faces the task of aligning its domestic policies with international climate goals and supporting global sustainability efforts. Through partnerships and knowledge-sharing initiatives, Germany contributes to international climate finance, technology transfer, and capacity-building programs. Participation in global agreements such as the Paris Agreement and the United Nations Sustainable Development Goals (SDGs) underscores Germany's commitment to global sustainability.

In conclusion, Germany's journey towards sustainability is marked by significant challenges that require innovative solutions and collaborative efforts. From advancing renewable energy integration and decarbonizing industry to promoting sustainable urban development and enhancing climate resilience, Germany continues to lead by example. By investing in research and development, leveraging digital technologies, and fostering public engagement, Germany is paving the way for a sustainable future. These efforts not only address current environmental challenges but also create opportunities for economic growth, social equity, and environmental protection.

9

The Future of Sustainability in Germany

As Germany continues to pioneer in the field of sustainability, the future holds significant potential for further advancements and global impact. This chapter speculates on and projects the future trajectory of Germany's sustainability efforts, considering technological innovations, policy developments, and their influence on global practices.

Germany's commitment to achieving climate neutrality by 2050 sets a clear path for its future sustainability endeavors. This ambitious goal will drive continued investment in renewable energy technologies, smart grids, and energy storage solutions. Solar and wind energy are expected to dominate the energy landscape, with advancements in efficiency and storage capabilities making these sources more reliable and widespread. Innovations such as floating wind farms and high-efficiency solar panels could become commonplace, further reducing dependence on fossil fuels.

The integration of renewable energy into the national grid will be supported by cutting-edge technologies like artificial intelligence (AI) and the Internet of Things (IoT). Smart grids, enhanced by AI, will optimize energy distribution, balance supply and demand, and manage storage systems more effectively. IoT devices will enable real-time monitoring and control of energy consumption, contributing to a more efficient and resilient energy infrastructure.

In the industrial sector, Germany's focus on green hydrogen is poised to revolutionize heavy industry and transportation. Green hydrogen, produced through electrolysis using renewable energy, offers a clean alternative to fossil fuels. As production costs decrease and infrastructure expands, green hydrogen is expected to power industrial processes, long-haul transportation, and even residential heating. Germany's leadership in this technology could spur global adoption, particularly in sectors where electrification is challenging.

The transportation sector will continue its transformation towards sustainability. Electric vehicles (EVs) are projected to dominate the market, supported by a comprehensive network of charging stations and advancements in battery technology. Autonomous electric vehicles and electric public transport systems will become more prevalent, reducing emissions and improving urban mobility. Hydrogen fuel cell vehicles may also gain traction, especially for heavy-duty and long-distance applications.

Urban planning in Germany will increasingly emphasize sustainability, with smart cities becoming the norm. These cities will integrate renewable energy, green infrastructure, and digital technologies to enhance quality of life while reducing environmental impact. Urban areas will feature extensive green spaces, vertical gardens, and eco-friendly buildings with advanced insulation and energy-efficient systems. Public transportation will be seamless and efficient, reducing the need for private car ownership.

Germany's circular economy initiatives will further evolve, minimizing waste and maximizing resource efficiency. Advances in recycling technologies, such as chemical recycling, will enable the recovery of more types of materials, reducing the environmental footprint of products. The concept of a sharing economy will gain prominence, with shared services for mobility, tools, and appliances becoming widespread. Product-as-a-service models, where consumers lease rather than own products, will promote sustainability and reduce waste.

Germany's agricultural practices will also undergo significant changes to enhance sustainability. Precision agriculture, utilizing drones, sensors, and AI, will optimize resource use, improve crop yields, and reduce environmental impact. Sustainable farming practices, such as agroforestry and regenerative agriculture, will become more common, enhancing soil health and biodiversity. Urban agriculture and vertical farming will contribute to local food production, reducing the carbon footprint associated with food transport.

Public engagement and education will remain critical to the success of Germany's sustainability efforts. Schools, universities, and community organizations will continue to promote environmental awareness and sustainable practices. Digital platforms and social media will play a key role in disseminating information, encouraging citizen participation, and fostering a culture of sustainability. Grassroots movements and community initiatives will thrive, driving local action and innovation.

Germany's leadership in sustainability will have a profound impact on global practices. As a technological and policy innovator, Germany will serve as a model for other nations, demonstrating the feasibility and benefits of a sustainable economy. International collaborations and knowledge-sharing initiatives will facilitate the global spread of best practices and technologies. Germany's participation in global climate agreements and its financial support for developing countries will help drive worldwide progress towards sustainability.

In conclusion, the future of sustainability in Germany is marked by continued innovation, ambitious goals, and a commitment to environmental stewardship. Through advancements in renewable energy, green hydrogen, smart urban planning, and circular economy practices, Germany will lead the way in creating a sustainable and resilient future. These efforts will not only enhance the well-being of its citizens but also contribute to global sustainability, setting a powerful example for the rest of the world.

10

• *Introduction: Germany's Path to Sustainability*

Germany has long been recognized as a global leader in environmental protection and sustainability. This commitment is deeply rooted in the nation's policies, practices, and cultural ethos, reflecting a comprehensive approach to preserving the environment while fostering economic growth. Germany's journey towards sustainability began in the late 20th century, catalyzed by growing environmental awareness and the urgent need to address pollution and resource depletion. The country's Green Party, established in 1980, played a crucial role in bringing environmental issues to the forefront of political discourse. Over the years, this focus on sustainability has permeated various levels of governance, from local municipalities to federal institutions.

Central to Germany's sustainability efforts is a robust policy framework designed to promote environmental stewardship across all sectors. Key legislative measures include the Renewable Energy Sources Act (EEG), enacted in 2000, which has been instrumental in transitioning Germany's energy sector towards renewable sources. It mandates preferential grid access for renewable energy producers and guarantees fixed feed-in tariffs, encouraging investment in wind, solar, and biomass energy. The Climate Action Plan 2050, launched in 2016, outlines Germany's long-term strategy to achieve greenhouse gas neutrality by 2050. It sets interim targets for 2030 and 2040, emphasizing energy efficiency, sustainable transportation, and carbon pricing mechanisms. The Circular Economy Act focuses on waste reduction, recycling, and resource efficiency, aiming to minimize landfill use and promote the reuse of materials, aligning with the principles of a circular economy.

Germany's commitment to renewable energy is evident in its ambitious Energiewende (energy transition) initiative. This multi-decade project seeks to overhaul the national energy system, reducing dependency on fossil fuels and nuclear power. Key achievements include Germany becoming one of the world's leading producers of wind energy, with extensive onshore and offshore wind farms harnessing the country's favorable wind conditions, particularly in the North Sea and Baltic Sea regions. Significant strides in solar energy have been made, with widespread adoption of photovoltaic systems. Rooftop solar panels are a common sight in German cities, contributing to decentralized energy production. To complement renewable energy generation, Germany invests in advanced energy storage solutions and smart grid technologies, enhancing grid stability and ensuring a reliable supply of clean energy.

Germany's automotive industry is undergoing a transformative shift towards sustainable mobility. Leading car manufacturers are increasingly focusing on electric and hybrid vehicles, driven by stringent emissions regulations and changing consumer preferences. Additionally, the government supports the expansion of public transportation networks and the development of cycling infrastructure, promoting low-carbon commuting options. Germany places a strong emphasis on preserving biodiversity and natural habitats, boasting numerous protected areas, including national parks, nature reserves, and biosphere reserves. Conservation initiatives prioritize the protection of endangered species, sustainable forestry practices, and the restoration of degraded ecosystems.

Public awareness and education are critical components of Germany's sustainability strategy. The government, alongside non-governmental organizations, conducts extensive campaigns to inform citizens about environmental issues and sustainable practices. Educational institutions at all levels integrate sustainability into their curricula, fostering a culture of environmental responsibility from an early age. Germany's commitment to sustainability extends beyond its borders, positioning the country as a key player in global environmental governance. It actively participates in international agreements, such as the Paris Agreement, and collaborates with other nations to address climate change and promote sustainable development. German expertise in renewable energy and environmental technologies is widely sought after, contributing to global efforts to combat environmental challenges.

Germany's path to sustainability is characterized by a comprehensive and integrated approach, encompassing policy innovation, technological advancement, and public engagement. As the country continues to lead by example, its commitment to environmental protection and sustainability serves as a blueprint for other nations striving to balance economic growth with ecological stewardship.

11

Energiewende – The Renewable Energy Revolution

Germany's Energiewende, or "energy transition," represents one of the most ambitious and comprehensive efforts to shift a major industrialized nation from reliance on fossil fuels to renewable energy sources. This chapter delves into the multifaceted aspects of Germany's energy transformation, exploring its origins, key policies, technological advancements, challenges, and future prospects.

The concept of Energiewende emerged in the late 20th century, driven by growing concerns over environmental degradation, climate change, and energy security. The 1970s oil crises, coupled with the rising environmental movement, highlighted the vulnerabilities associated with fossil fuel dependency. These events spurred public and political support for alternative energy solutions, laying the groundwork for Germany's energy revolution.

Central to Energiewende is the Renewable Energy Sources Act (EEG), enacted in 2000. This landmark legislation aimed to promote the development and integration of renewable energy by providing fixed feed-in tariffs and guaranteeing grid access for renewable energy producers. The EEG has been instrumental in catalyzing investment in wind, solar, biomass, and other renewable technologies, making Germany a global leader in renewable energy capacity.

Wind power plays a pivotal role in Germany's renewable energy portfolio. The country's geographic location, with its extensive coastlines along the North Sea and Baltic Sea, offers favorable conditions for both onshore and offshore wind farms. Germany has become one of the world's top producers of wind energy, with significant contributions from large-scale offshore installations. These projects harness strong and consistent winds, providing a reliable and substantial source of clean energy.

Solar energy also constitutes a significant component of Germany's Energiewende. The widespread adoption of photovoltaic systems, supported by government incentives and technological advancements, has led to the proliferation of solar panels on rooftops and solar farms across the country. Despite Germany's relatively modest solar irradiance compared to sunnier regions, the efficiency and scalability of solar technology have enabled substantial growth in solar energy production.

Complementing the expansion of renewable energy generation are advancements in energy storage and smart grid technologies. Energy storage solutions, such as batteries and pumped hydro storage, address the intermittency of renewable sources by storing excess energy for use during periods of low generation. Smart grids enhance the flexibility and stability of the electricity system, enabling efficient distribution and integration of renewable energy into the national grid. These innovations are crucial for maintaining a reliable and resilient energy infrastructure.

Germany's commitment to reducing greenhouse gas emissions and enhancing energy efficiency is reflected in its Climate Action Plan 2050. This strategic framework outlines long-term goals for decarbonizing various sectors, including energy, transportation, and industry. The plan emphasizes the importance of energy efficiency measures, such as building insulation, energy-efficient appliances, and industrial process improvements. By reducing energy consumption, Germany aims to achieve a more sustainable and cost-effective energy system.

The transition to renewable energy also entails significant socio-economic implications. The shift away from fossil fuels has created new opportunities for green jobs and industries, contributing to economic growth and innovation. However, it has also posed challenges, particularly for regions and communities historically dependent on coal and other fossil fuels. Managing this transition requires careful planning and support for affected workers and industries, ensuring a just and equitable shift towards a sustainable energy future.

Despite its successes, Energiewende faces several challenges. The intermittency of renewable energy sources necessitates robust storage and grid management solutions. Balancing energy supply and demand, especially during periods of high renewable generation, requires advanced forecasting and flexible energy systems. Additionally, the integration of decentralized renewable energy sources into the existing grid infrastructure demands substantial investment and coordination.

Looking ahead, Germany's Energiewende continues to evolve, with ongoing efforts to enhance the efficiency, reliability, and sustainability of its energy system. The country's leadership in renewable energy innovation and policy serves as a model for other nations pursuing similar transitions. As global efforts to combat climate change intensify, Germany's experience offers valuable insights into the complexities and opportunities of transforming an energy system towards a sustainable future.

In conclusion, Germany's Energiewende represents a transformative journey towards a renewable energy future. Through visionary policies, technological innovation, and public engagement, Germany has demonstrated the feasibility and benefits of transitioning from fossil fuels to renewable energy sources. This energy revolution not only addresses environmental and climate challenges but also fosters economic resilience and sustainability, paving the way for a cleaner and more prosperous future.